monday morning®

FOR THE LOVE OF
Sentences

By Murray Suid
Illustrated by Corbin Hillam

This book is for Anne Diskin.

Publisher: Roberta Suid
Editor: Elizabeth Russell
Cover Design: David Hale
Design and Production: Susan Pinkerton
Cover Art: Corbin Hillam

monday morning®

Monday Morning is a registered trademark
of Monday Morning Books, Inc.

Entire contents copyright © 1986 by Monday Morning
Books, Inc., Box 1680, Palo Alto, California 94302

Permission is hereby granted to reproduce
student materials in this book for non-commercial
individual or classroom use.

ISBN 0-912107-51-0

Printed in the United States of America

9 8 7 6 5 4 3 2

Contents

Part I. Skills

Sentence Fundamentals — 5
   The Sentence Play — 6
   Subjects and Predicates — 12
   Declarative Sentences — 13
   Imperative Sentences — 14
   Interrogative Sentences — 15
   Exclamatory Sentences — 16
   Sentence Sorting — 17
   Sentence Collecting — 18
   Turning Fragments into Sentences — 19
   Combining Sentences — 20
   Dividing Sentences — 21
   Untangling run-on Sentences — 22

Parts of speech — 23
   Parts of Speech Speeches — 24
   Two Way Parts of Speech — 26
   Word-o Cards — 27
   Bulletin Board — 28

Punctuation — 29
   Punctuation Speeches — 30
   Punctuation Collecting — 32

Paragraphs — 33
   Paragraph Speeches — 34
   Building Paragraphs — 35
   Connection Questions — 36
   Find the Paragraphs — 37
   Linking Paragraphs — 38

Part II. Projects

Bulletin Board — 39
ABC Sentences — 40
About-me Sentences — 42
Add-a-word Sentences — 44
Bumper Stickers — 46
Captions — 48
Definitions — 50
Digests — 52
Far-out Sentences — 54
Mottoes and Slogans — 56
My Words Only Game — 58
Numbered Stories and Essays — 59
Parts-of-speech Poems — 60
Pass-it-on Sentences — 61
Single Sentence Picture Books — 62

Introduction

> I set a realistic objective: How can I inch along to the next paragraph? Inching is what it is.—Joseph Heller

If you want quality writing, you've got to have well-made sentences. Unfortunately, students sometimes ignore these "mini-compositions" as they rush to complete their stories, reports, and other projects. The result is predictable: unclear and uninteresting work.

Here's where *For the Love of Sentences* can help. This book presents effective, motivating, yet simple-to-manage activities that will help you teach young writers to:
- value the craft of sentence writing,
- understand the basic forms and uses of sentences,
- master the parts of speech,
- punctuate correctly,
- use grammatical knowledge for editing their work, and
- link sentences effectively to produce paragraphs.

Part I—Skills — presents the fundamentals of sentences and paragraphs. You will find lessons and *reproducible worksheets* dealing with sentence structure (subjects and predicates), parts of speech, punctuation, paragraphing, and editing.

Part II—Projects — provides a collection of imaginative writing tasks. These exercises will help students develop their basic skills while turning out works of real value—for example, school and classroom mottoes.

A number of the activities are reusable. Many require only a few minutes and can serve as warm-ups or "sponge projects" that turn spare moments into meaningful learning experiences. You might also send some of the sentence and paragraph games home for parents and children to enjoy as after-dinner "edutainment." Two examples are "About-me Sentences" and "My Words Only."

The goal is simple: As students come to understand, appreciate, and master the sentence, their longer assignments will gain in power, clarity, and creativity.

Happy writing.

© 1986 Monday Morning Books, Inc.

Sentence Fundamentals

GOAL:
Becoming familiar with sentence fundamentals

ACTIVITIES:
1. Use *The Sentence Play worksheets* to present the key ideas of sentence structure. Students might simply read aloud the six pages. Another option is to perform the skit in costumes for other classes. Later, you can reinforce the basic concepts with the *Subjects and Predicates worksheet*.
2. For practice with the four types of sentences, hand out the *Declarative Sentences, Imperative Sentences, Interrogative Sentences,* and *Exclamatory Sentences* worksheets. Two related worksheets—*Sentence Sorting* and *Sentence Collecting*—link the earlier lessons to actual sentences found in books, magazines, and other works.
3. Relate sentence mastery to the essential skill of editing with the final worksheets in this section—*Turning Fragments into Sentences, Combining Sentences, Dividing Sentences,* and *Untangling Run-on Sentences*.
4. Extend the editing activities beyond the given worksheets. For example, once students know how to combine sentences, have them practice this skill on a regular basis using examples created by the teacher or by classmates.

© 1986 Monday Morning Books, Inc.

The Sentence Play

The action could happen any place where a pencil, a piece of paper, and a few words might get together.

Characters

Note: Characters in quotation marks are words. For example, "I" stands for the word *I*. When appearing on stage, these word characters might wear shirts or placards printed with their names.

Pencil	"Flowers"	Question mark
Paper	"Like"	"Smell"
"I"	Period	"These"
"Pretty"	"Do"	Exclamation point

Paper: (Enters.) Hello, Pencil. Were you looking for me?

Pencil: Yes, I was, Paper.

Paper: How can I help you?

Pencil: I do a lot of writing, and people tell me that anyone who writes needs to know about sentences.

Paper: That's true. Whether you're working on a story, a report, a letter, or almost any writing job, you share your ideas sentence by sentence. If your sentences are weak or confused, what you write won't be clear or interesting.

© 1986 Monday Morning Books, Inc.

The Sentence Play

Pencil: How can I learn to write good sentences?

Paper: I think I can help you because I've seen many sentences in my life.

Pencil: Where do we begin?

Paper: First, you need to know what a sentence is.

Pencil: Isn't a sentence just a group of words?

Paper: Not really. You can have a group of words that aren't a sentence. (Paper claps its hands.)

(Three words — "I," "pretty," and "flowers" — enter and stand in the order shown below.)

Pencil: (Reads the words.) "I pretty flowers."

Paper: Do you notice anything strange about that group of words?

Pencil: It doesn't mean anything.

Paper: You're right. To be a sentence a group of words must make sense.

© 1986 Monday Morning Books, Inc.

The Sentence Play

Pencil: (Turns to the words.) Go away, words. We don't need you. We're looking for words that make sense.

Words: Boo hoo. (They start to leave.)

Paper: Hold on! These words can make sense, but something is missing. Every sentence needs at least two main parts: a subject and a predicate. If it doesn't have both parts, it's called a sentence fragment.

Pencil: What's a subject?

Paper: The subject is what the sentence is about. It's like the star of a movie. In this group of words, there is a subject. It's the word "I."

"I": ("I" takes a bow.)

Pencil: Now explain what a predicate is?

Paper: The predicate tells what's going on. It always includes a verb, which is an action word. (Paper claps its hands.)

"Like": (The word "like" appears and squeezes in between pretty and flowers.)

8 © 1986 Monday Morning Books, Inc.

The Sentence Play

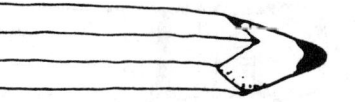

Pencil: (Reads the words.) "I pretty like flowers." Hmm, that still doesn't make sense.

Paper: That's because the words are in the wrong order. In a sentence, the order of words is very important.

Pencil: Couldn't we just move them around?

Paper: Good idea. Would "like," please go between "I" and "pretty"?

"Like": (The word "like" moves between "I" and "pretty.") Here?

Pencil: (Reads the words.) "I like pretty flowers." That sounds much better.

Paper: Yes, but there's still one thing missing.

Pencil: What?

Paper: When you write a sentence, you need to let readers know where it ends.

Pencil: How do you do that?

Paper: With punctuation marks. (Paper claps hands again.)

Period: (Period enters.) Where should I go?

Paper: Over there, to the right of "flowers." (Pauses.) Perfect.

Pencil: Thanks a lot, Paper. Now I understand everything about sentences.

Paper: I wouldn't say everything.

Pencil: What else is there?

Paper: For one thing, you should know that there are four kinds of sentences. Each does a different job.

Pencil: Is that so? I'm amazed! I'll never be able to learn that. Don't even try to teach me.

Paper: Do you want to know something?

© 1986 Monday Morning Books, Inc.

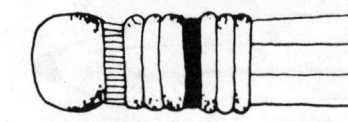

The Sentence Play

Pencil: What?

Paper: You just used all four kinds of sentences.

Pencil: Really?

Paper: Sure. Let me explain. When you simply want to give someone some information, you do that with a declarative sentence. *Declare* means *to tell*.

Pencil: Can you give me an example?

Paper: There's one standing right in front of you. It's the sentence "I like pretty flowers."

Pencil: I see. It does gives information.

Paper: We can change that into a question sentence—called an interrogative—by adding a word and a question mark. (Claps.)

"Do": (Enters the stage and stands to the left of "I.")

Question mark: (Enters the stage and takes Period's place. Period moves off to one side.)

Pencil: (Reads the new sentence): "Do I like pretty flowers?" That sentence certainly asks a question.

The Sentence Play

Paper: If you're ready, I'll change it into a sentence that gives directions or orders. It's called an imperative. (Claps.)

"Smell" & "These": (The words "Do," "I," and "like" move off to one side making room for "Smell" and "these." Period moves to the end of the sentence and Question mark exits.

Pencil: (Reads the sentence): "Smell these pretty flowers." That sentence is now giving *orders* and not just *odors*.

Paper: If that was a joke, I forgive you for it. Let's just turn this into an exclamatory sentence—one that shows excitement. We need an exclamation point. (Claps.)

Exclamation point: (Exclamation point replaces the period, which exits.)

Pencil: (Reads the sentence loudly): "Smell these pretty flowers!" I think I understand the four kinds of sentences. But what's the use of having all four? Tell me. Please tell me!

Paper: The reason is simple. Writers often want to share information. Other times, they need to ask their readers a question. Sometimes, they want to give directions. And finally, they might choose to show excitement. To do these things, they need the four kinds of sentences.

Pencil: Now, do I know everything about sentences?

Paper: (Shakes its head.) I'm afraid not. But you have a good start. One of the best ways to learn more is to pay attention to sentences when you read and when you write.

Pencil: I see your point.

Paper: And I see yours. Goodbye.

The End

© 1986 Monday Morning Books, Inc.

Subjects and Predicates

Every sentence has two main parts—a subject and a predicate. The *subject* is like the star of a movie. It tells who or what the sentence is about. The *predicate* is like the action of the movie. It explains what the subject does or what happens to the subject.

1. Add a predicate to each of the following subjects in order to make a complete sentence. A sample has been done for you.

A. The wolf *chased the rabbit.*

B. My friend _____

C. The big storm _____

D. Seven hungry giants _____

E. The frozen lake _____

F. A mean-looking cat _____

2. Add a subject to each of the following predicates to make a complete sentence. Again, a sample has been done for you.

A. *The two tiny dogs* tried to scare us.

B. _____ walked up the hill.

C. _____ made a terrible noise.

D. _____ was never seen again.

E. _____ could not tell a lie.

F. _____ flew over the building.

G. _____ smiled in a scary way.

Declarative Sentences

A sentence that tells what the writer sees, knows, or believes is called a *declarative* sentence. "Declarative" comes from the word "declare," which means "tell" or "say."

Write as many declarative sentences as you can about the picture on this page. A sample has been done for you. (If you need more space, use another piece of paper.)

The picture is upside down.

© 1986 Monday Morning Books, Inc.

Imperative Sentences

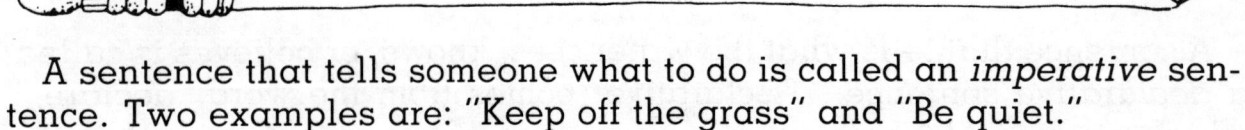

A sentence that tells someone what to do is called an *imperative* sentence. Two examples are: "Keep off the grass" and "Be quiet."

1. Write a sentence that goes with each picture. Use imperative (direction-giving) sentences.

HOW TO WASH YOUR DOG

2. On the back of this page write a set of directions for an everyday activity. The task could be getting dressed, brushing your teeth, making your bed, or preparing some kind of food. If you like, draw pictures that help explain each step of the directions.

Interrogative Sentences

A sentence that asks a question is called an *interrogative* sentence. Learning to think up interesting questions will help you become a better student and a better writer.

1. Write as many questions as you can about this picture. A sample has been done for you. If you need more space, use the back of this sheet.

Where is he going?

_____

_____

_____

2. Write a question about each of the following sentences. The first one has been done for you.

A. My friend is learning to speak French.

_____

B. Everyone was afraid of the machine.

_____

C. I had looked everywhere.

_____

D. No one had touched a bite of the food.

_____

3. Write a question that no one in your class could answer except you. It might be about a friend or a place you've visited.

_____

_____

© 1986 Monday Morning Books, Inc.

15

Exclamatory Sentences

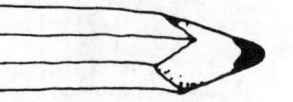

A sentence that shows excitement is called an *exclamatory* sentence. "Exclamatory" comes from the word "exclaim," which means to cry out.

Fill in the balloons in the scene below with exclamatory sentences. An example has been done for you.

I CAN WALK ON MY HANDS!

PLEASE GIVE THE GRASS A CHANCE.

Sentence Sorting

In the picture below find one or more of the following kinds of sentences.

1. Declarative sentences (they give facts or opinions)

___

2. Interrogative sentences (they ask questions)

___

3. Imperative sentences (they give commands)

___

4. Exclamatory sentences (they show excitement)

___

5. Sentence fragments (they're missing the subject or the predicate)

___

© 1986 Monday Morning Books, Inc.

Sentence Collecting

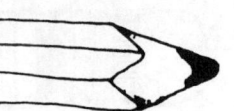

If you want to write interesting sentences, learn to notice different kinds of sentences when you read. Start today. In the boxes below write at least one example of each kind of sentence. Look for the examples in books, newspapers, magazines, or even on signs. Tell where you found each one.

Declarative sentences

Interrogative sentences

Imperative sentences

Exclamatory sentences

© 1986 Monday Morning Books, Inc.

Turning Fragments into Sentences

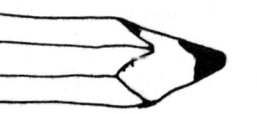

A sentence without a complete subject or predicate is called a sentence fragment. Newspaper writers sometimes use sentence fragments as headlines to save space.

1. Rewrite each of the following headlines as a complete sentence. You may need to add some words or cross out others. Be sure to include the correct punctuation mark. A sample has been done for you.

A. Peace talks planned

Peace talks are planned.

B. New zoo to open soon

_____

C. Subway crime a growing problem

_____

D. Food costs up

_____

E. Baseball players on strike

_____

F. Rain tonight

_____

G. Money problems?

_____

2. On the back of this paper, write two or three headlines from your town's newspaper. If the headlines are fragments, rewrite them as sentences.

© 1986 Monday Morning Books, Inc.

Combining Sentences

Your writing will usually be more interesting if it includes both short and long sentences. If something you have written has mostly short sentences, you can easily fix it. Simply combine some of the short sentences.

1. Rewrite each pair of short sentences as one longer sentence. To connect the sentences, use the words below. You may need to leave out a word. The first one has been done for you.

after, although, and, because, but, unless, when

A. Thunder shook the room. I closed my eyes.

When thunder shook the room, I closed my eyes.

B. I like dogs. They are fun to play with.

_____

C. Some people enjoy summer best. Winter is my favorite season.

_____

D. I walked in the rain. Then I started sneezing.

_____

E. Will you let me play? If you don't, I'll go home.

_____

2. Join all three sentences into one longer sentence. You can leave out words, but use no more than one "and" in a sentence.

A. I can run. I can jump. I can swim.

_____

B. Mrs. Springer teaches here. Mr. Jordan teaches here. Mr. Nolan teaches here, too.

_____

3. On the back write two short sentences. Then write them as one sentence.

20

© 1986 Monday Morning Books, Inc.

Dividing Sentences

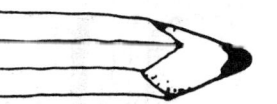

Long sentences can be interesting. However, an overlong sentence may confuse your readers. If you find a sentence like that, try dividing it.

1. Rewrite each of the following sentences as two or more shorter sentences. You may need to add words to make the meaning clear.

A. I went to the ball game with my friends, and we had good seats and afterwards we went out for dinner and enjoyed our food.

_____
_____
_____

B. When my grandparents were my age, they didn't watch TV because TV hadn't been invented, so instead they would listen to programs on the radio, and their favorites were "The Lone Ranger" and "The Shadow."

_____
_____
_____

C. I have many pets including goldfish, two cats, a dog, a snake, and a mouse which sometimes gets out of its cage, and when that happens, my family gets angry with me and then I run around trying to catch the mouse, and that isn't an easy thing to do.

_____
_____
_____

2. On the back of this sheet, write a sentence that has at least 15 words. Then rewrite that sentence as two or more shorter sentences.

© 1986 Monday Morning Books, Inc.

Untangling Run-on Sentences

Every sentence needs a clear ending. If it doesn't have one, it can seem to be part of the next sentence. When that happens, it's called a "run-on sentence." Because run-on sentences confuse readers, you need to know what to do about them.

1. One way to fix a run-on sentence is to break it into two sentences. Do that with the following examples. Put a period or a question mark where the first sentence ends. Circle the mark. Also, be sure to start the second sentence with a capital letter. A sample has been done for you.

A. My friend likes to swim(.)~~m~~My favorite sport is basketball.

B. Did you find the book I was looking for it was on the table.

C. The bike contest takes place tomorrow did you know that?

D. The new TV show made me laugh I'm glad I watched it.

E. My pet likes to bark that's unusual since he's a cat.

2. You can also fix run-on sentences by rewriting them. Try that here. The first one has been done for you.

A. You hit the ball farther than anyone who taught you how to bat?

Who taught you to hit the ball farther than anyone?

B. Here's my new camera if you want, I'll take a photograph of you.

___

C. Why did the lights go out was it because of the storm?

___

D. Run-on sentences are hard to read that's why they should be fixed.

___

Parts of Speech

GOAL:
Learning that every word in a sentence has a specific job to play

ACTIVITIES:
1. The *Parts-of-Speech Speeches worksheets* provide ready-to-deliver lectures that students can perform in small groups or for the entire class.
2. The *Parts-of-Speech Bulletin Board* visually reinforces the concepts taught in the previous activity. Students can help create these bulletin boards by collecting or drawing the illustrations suggested in the teaching tips.
3. The *Two-way Words worksheet* teaches the idea that a word's function depends on its context.
4. In the Word-O game, students identify parts of speech in sentences taken from published material or from class papers. To start, the leader writes a sentence on the board. Players then copy words from the sentence into appropriate boxes on their Word-O cards. The leader then writes another sentence on the board. The first player to complete a row, column, or diagonal calls out "Word-O." Two sample cards appear on the *Word-O worksheet*. Students can make additional Word-O cards with the parts of speech in different arrangements.
5. Another enjoyable way to learn about parts of speech is playing Mad Libs, a fill-in-the-blank game. You can buy ready-to-use Mad Lib booklets at most greeting card and novelty shops. (The publisher is Price, Stern, and Sloan.) Using these as models, students can make up their own Mad Lib sheets.

© 1986 Monday Morning Books, Inc.

Parts-of-Speech Speeches

I am a *noun*. My job is to name people, places, and things. When you ask a question that starts with *who* or *what*, the answer is usually a noun.

"Who flies an airplane?" The answer is the noun *pilot*.

"What do you sleep in?" The answer is the noun *bed*

If you want to name your pet, your favorite food, what you wear, your friends, the games you play, you need nouns.

Everything that you can see or touch is a noun. In other words, there are lots of nouns in your life.

I am a *verb*. You'll find at least one of me in every sentence. I tell what's going on.

If the sentence is about a cat, I let you know if the cat is *meowing* or *jumping* or *sleeping*. If the sentence is about a person, I might tell you that he or she is *thinking* or *laughing* or *talking*.

Some sentences don't have much action. They just give facts, for example, "The rock is heavy." Even in such a sentence, there's a place for me, because *is* is a verb.

As you can see, without me, nothing would happen.

I am an *adjective*. I help people learn more about whatever a noun has named.

For example, take the noun *pilot*. I might explain that the pilot is friendly and tall. *Friendly* and *tall* are adjectives.

Take the noun *bedroom*. Adjectives could show that the bedroom is neat, warm, and bright. And if the noun names a thing such as a car, adjectives might describe it as new, fast, and red.

Whenever you ask the question, "What kind of person, place or thing is it?" the answer will be an adjective.

I am an *adverb*. I help verbs tell what's happening. I do this by answering three questions: how, when, and where.

In the sentence — "The dog barks"—barks is the verb. How does the dog bark? Whether it barks *loudly* or *softly*, the answer is an adverb.

In the sentence—"The dog barked yesterday"—yesterday is an adverb that tells when the barking happened.

If the dog is barking outside, *outside* is an adverb, because it tells you where the barking is.

© 1986 Monday Morning Books, Inc.

Parts-of-Speech Speeches

I am a *conjunction*. I join words together. For example, the *and* in "peanut butter and jelly" is a conjunction.

And is the most popular conjunction, but it's not the only one. *But* gets a lot of use as well.

Take the sentence: "I want to draw, *but* I don't have a crayon." The word *but* joins "I want to draw" with "I don't have a crayon."

Other conjunctions include *or*, *if*, *although*, *when*, and *unless*.

I am a *preposition*. While *preposition* is a big word, most prepositions are short. Examples include *in*, *on*, *under*, *above*, *around*, *from*, and *over*.

Prepositions help explain where things are. For example, suppose that you've lost your keys. Wherever they are, a preposition will help you search for them.

Are the keys *on* the table, *under* the book, *in* the drawer, *around* the corner, or *behind* the toaster?

I am a *pronoun*. My job is to take the place of a noun.

Suppose you say, "I like to eat oranges, but I don't eat them every day." The word *them* is a pronoun which replaces the word *oranges*.

What good is a pronoun? You can hear for yourself by trying to say the sentence without the pronoun:

"I like to eat oranges, but I don't eat oranges every day."

Using *oranges* twice makes the sentence sound strange. The pronoun *them* lets you avoid repeating the word *oranges*.

There are many other pronouns. These include *I*, *we*, *you*, *he*, *she*, *it*, and *they*. You probably couldn't get along without any of *them*.

Wow! Gosh! Gee whiz! I like being an *interjection*. An interjection is a word that shows feeling.

Words like *whoopie* or *boo* don't really mean anything. But they let people know when you're happy, sad, angry, or—yikes!— surprised.

The interjection *hmmmm* can show that you're thinking. When you get the answer, if you want people to see that you've got it, just shout *aha!*

© 1986 Monday Morning Books, Inc.

Two-way Parts of Speech

Many things can be used in more than one way.

This is also true with words. In one sentence, a word may be used as a noun—for example, "I go to the *bank*." In another sentence, the same word may be an adjective—"Here's my *bank* book."

The more ways you can use a word, the better you'll be as a writer.

1. Label the part of speech of each of the underlined words. A sample has been done for you. Use these abbreviations:

   n. for noun (A noun names a person, place, or thing.)
   pron. for pronoun (A pronoun replaces a noun.)
   v. for verb (A verb shows action.)
   prep. for preposition (A preposition tells where something is.)
   adj. for adjective (An adjective gives facts about a noun.)
   conj. for conjunction (A conjunction joins words.)
   adv. for adverb (An adverb tells how or when something happens.)

       v.   adj.
   A. *Ski* down the hill to the *ski* lodge.

   B. I *wish* I had another *wish*.

   C. Let's *stop* at the bus *stop*.

   D. I'll *care* if you don't handle my money with *care*.

   E. Listen to the *music* from the *music* box.

   F. Who will *play* the hero in our class *play*?

   G. Wrap the food with a piece of plastic *wrap*.

   H. I will now *mix* the cake *mix*.

   I. Don't run *up* the *up* escalator.

2. On the back of this sheet, write sentences that use each of the following words as two different parts of speech: *tie* and *run*.

Word-O Cards

You'll find directions for using these Word-O cards on page 23. For a variety of cards, white out the abbreviations and write in other patterns of the parts of speech.

n.	conj.	adj.	adv.	prep.
adj.	prep.	n.	v.	n.
interj.	pron.	conj.	adv.	conj.
v.	n.	prep.	adj.	adj.
n.	conj.	v.	n.	adv.

conj.	adv.	v.	adj.	n.
n.	n.	pron.	interj.	adv.
adj.	adj.	n.	adv.	n.
n.	pron.	adv.	v.	conj.
conj.	pron.	adj.	v.	adj.

© 1986 Monday Morning Books, Inc.

27

Bulletin Board

Pictures or dramatic scenes can help students learn the parts of speech. Have the class draw or collect pictures for illustrating the other seven parts of speech bulletin boards. Some art ideas are:

noun—Label all the parts of an object such as a bicycle.

pronoun—Show a man with a T-shirt labeled "He," a woman with a T-shirt labeled "She," etc.

adjective—Show a robot labeled with adjectives like big, strong, scary, etc.

verb—Display a collection of magazine or newspaper photos showing actions. Label each picture with a verb—Run. Cry. Jump. Eat, etc.

adverb—Add an appropriate adverb to each of the above pictures, e.g., Eat quickly. Cry loudly. Jump gracefully.

conjunction—Show a bottle of glue. On the label print "and," "but," "or," and other conjunctions.

interjections—Collect pictures that show people being enthusiastic. Give each person a dialogue balloon with an interjection. For example, a cheerleader could be saying "Hurray!"

Punctuation

GOAL:
Increasing punctuation awareness

ACTIVITIES:
1. The *Punctuation Speeches worksheets* provide the text for lectures about periods, commas, and seven other basic marks.
2. The *Punctuation Collecting worksheet* reinforces basic punctuation knowledge by having students find examples in the real world of writing.

© 1986 Monday Morning Books, Inc.

Punctuation Speeches

I am the little dot known as a *period*. You'll find me at the end of any sentence that gives a fact or an opinion. When readers see me, they know it's time to get ready for a new idea.

Besides showing where sentences end, I'm also used in abbreviations. For example, if your middle name is Humberdingler, and Humberdingler takes up too much room, you can just write H period.

I am a *comma*, a period with a little tail. My job is to separate words or groups of words in a sentence. For example, if you list three of your hobbies in a sentence, you should use commas to separate them.

In the same way, I separate the name of a city and the state when you write an address.

One thing I *don't* do is join separate sentences. For example, suppose you write: "I like to eat peanut butter." Then you add, "I do not like to eat squid." You cannot use me alone to connect these two sentences.

I am an *exclamation point*! I am used to show excitement. If you're writing a story in which a character shouts for help, put me at the end of the sentence.

You'll see me a lot in advertisements. I help readers notice words like "Free!" or "Two for one!"

You have to be careful, though, when using me. If you end too many sentences with exclamation points, your readers will get bored.

Who am I? I am a *question mark*. What do I do? I show that someone is asking a question.

For example, the first thing I said to you was "Who am I?" That sentence asks a question, so if you were writing it, you'd put one of me at the end.

© 1986 Monday Morning Books, Inc.

Punctuation Speeches

I come in pairs. Can you guess my name? I'm *quotation marks*.

Story writers put me before and after the words their characters say. This separates the characters' talk from the rest of the story.

I am used in another way. When you write the title of a short story, a newspaper article, or a song, put that name inside quotation marks.

I am the *colon*. I look like two periods, one above the other.

You'll often see me in the greeting in a business letter, right after the words "Dear Mr. Sloop" or "Dear Mrs. Parsley."

I am also used in a sentence that contains a list. Put me right before the list begins. Here's an example: "I have three hobbies (colon): sky-diving, snake charming, and mountain climbing."

I am a *semicolon*. I look like a comma with a period over it.

I have one big job to do in a sentence. You can use me to join two separate ideas instead of using a comma and a conjunction like *and* or *but*.

Take the sentences "I like to watch TV, but I don't like to listen to radio."

Instead of that, you could write: "I like to watch TV; I don't like to listen to radio."

I am *parentheses*. Like quotation marks, I always come in pairs. Part of me looks like the left half of a circle. The other part looks like the right half.

Together, we can mark a part of a sentence that is less important than the rest of the sentence. We tell readers that they don't have to pay as much attention to the words between us.

Punctuation Collecting

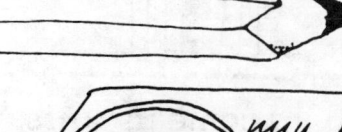

Always pay attention to punctuation marks when you are reading. This will help you when it's time for you to punctuate your own writing.

1. Try to find examples of each of the following punctuation marks. You can look in books, newspapers, magazines, and elsewhere. Write the examples in the spaces below and tell where you found them.

Period
Comma
Exclamation point
Question mark
Quotation marks
Colon
Semicolon
Parentheses
Underlining

2. If you find other punctuation marks, list them on the back and include an example for each.

Paragraphs

GOAL:
Learning how sentences link to form paragraphs

ACTIVITIES:
1. Use the *Paragraph Speeches worksheet* to define the basic paragraph concepts: main idea, supporting detail, indentation, and transitions.
2. Introduce the concept that paragraphs are built around main ideas with the *Building Paragraphs worksheet*. But don't stop with this one worksheet. Real mastery requires repetition. Therefore, on a regular basis—perhaps once a week — have the class practice adding details to a single topic sentence or to a main idea expressed in two sentences. Instead of having the teacher create all the paragraph starters, for more involvement sometimes ask students to provide each other with main ideas to elaborate.
3. Give students practice in linking sentences with the *Connection Questions worksheet*. Later, you might have students look for similar "hidden" questions in stories and articles they're reading, and in their own work as well.
4. Relate paragraphing to editing by having students mark the needed indentations on the *Find the Paragraphs worksheet*. To repeat this important exercise, you can make additional worksheets simply by copying stories or articles in un-paragraphed form.
   Note: In many cases, there isn't one right place to start a new paragraph. Even experienced editors will disagree. What's most important is for students to give reasons for their indentations, for example, by pointing out that a given sentence introduces a new subject or adds an example that needs to be dealt with by itself.
5. Introduce the idea of paragraph transitions with the *Linking Paragraphs worksheet*.

© 1986 Monday Morning Books, Inc.

Paragraph Speeches

I am a *paragraph*. I'm part of a story or report just the way a chapter is part of a book. Writers break their work into paragraphs to make the reader's job easier.

Sometimes a paragraph is just one word. Other times it can be as long as a page. Usually, though, a paragraph will contain between three and ten sentences.

Most paragraphs have one main idea. All of the sentences in the paragraph help explain that idea.

When you see the first line of a paragraph moved a little to the right, that's me you're looking at. You can call me *indentation*.

My job is simple, but it's important. I let the reader know that a new paragraph is about to begin. This makes it easier for the reader to understand what's going on.

I also make a page more pleasant to look at. Without me, the page would be one big glob of words. Indentations give the reader a break, like a rest area on a highway.

I am a *topic sentence*. I give the main idea of a paragraph. I might present an important fact, for example, that there are nine planets in the solar system. The other sentences in my paragraph might then explain something about the nine planets.

In an action story, the topic sentence might describe the setting. Then the other sentences could tell what happened there.

Usually, the topic sentence is the first sentence in the paragraph. It doesn't have to come first, but putting it there makes it easier for the reader to understand the paragraph.

I'm a *transition*. I work like a sign to guide readers from one paragraph to the next.

Imagine that you're writing a paper about friendship. Suppose your first paragraph explains that you have many good friends. Your second paragraph might be about one of those friends. You could begin that second paragraph with the words *For example*. These words show how the second paragraph grows from the first.

Other transitional words and phrases are *of course*, *next*, *however*, and *on the other hand*.

Building Paragraphs

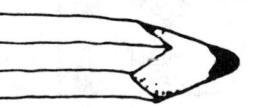

A paragraph is a group of sentences that deal with a main idea. Often, one sentence—called the topic sentence—will give the main idea. The other sentences will explain or support it by adding details or examples.

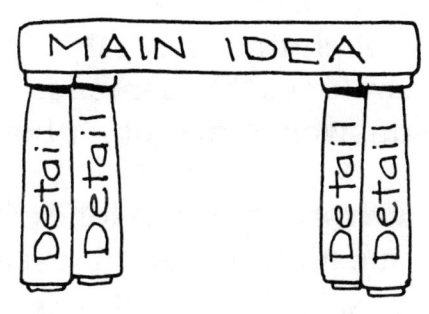

Complete each topic sentence. Then build a paragraph by writing two or three sentences that add details or examples.

1. My favorite food is _____.

_____

_____

_____

2. If I could visit any place in the world, it would be _____

_____.

_____

_____

_____

3. Once I saw a _____.

_____

_____

_____

4. If I could be any animal, I would choose to be a _____.

_____

_____

_____

© 1986 Monday Morning Books, Inc.

Connection Questions

A chain is built link by link. In the same way, writers build paragraphs sentence by sentence. One way to do this is to have each sentence answer a question about the sentence that came before it.

1. In each of the following examples, write a sentence that answers the question in parentheses. A sample has been done for you.

A. Today is my birthday. (So what?)
What are you planning to do?

B. I want to watch TV tonight. (Why?)
_____

C. A big bear escaped from the zoo this morning. (What happened next?)
_____

D. My friend just found a box full of gold. (Where?)
_____

E. I had a scary dream last night. (What was it?)
_____

F. My pencil just broke. (What else has gone wrong?)
_____

2. Write a question for each of the following sentences. Then write a sentence that answers the question.

A. This is my favorite book. (_____?)
_____

B. No one expected the big storm. (_____?)
_____

C. I just found my missing shoe. (_____?)
_____

3. Write a paragraph on a subject you know a lot about. After each sentence, write a question in parentheses ( ). Then answer that question in the next sentence.

36   © 1986 Monday Morning Books, Inc.

Find the Paragraphs

When you first write a paper, it may come out in one block of words. Later, when you edit your work, you will need to break it into paragraphs for easier reading.

1. Break the following story into three or four paragraphs. Put this mark (¶) wherever you think a new paragraph should begin.

Photography was invented over a hundred years ago. Back then some people called it "painting with the sun." Sunlight did the job of the paint. The film inside the camera acted like the canvas. This simple way of talking about photography still makes sense. Now, you may wonder exactly how the picture gets made. Everything starts when light enters the camera through the lens and hits the film. Like a piece of bread and jam, film has two parts. The "bread" part of the film, made of clear plastic, is called the base. It holds the "jam" part, called the *emulsion*. There are two main kinds of emulsions. One is for black and white photos, the other for color. Each works in the same basic way. The emulsion is *light sensitive*. This means that it changes when light hits it. You can't see the changes in the emulsion right away. You have to use chemicals that bring out the picture. This is called *developing the film*. Years ago, film developing had to be done outside the camera. You could develop it in a dark room in your house or take it to a photo lab. Today, however, many cameras use film with the developing chemicals built in. This way you get to see the pictures right away.

2. Compare your paragraph marks with someone else in the room. If you disagree where a new paragraph should start, give your reasons. Both of you might be right. Even famous writers may disagree about where to begin or end a paragraph.

Linking Paragraphs

Every writer must learn how to continue an idea from one paragraph to the next. Here's your chance to practice.

1. In each of the following examples, continue the idea that was started in the first paragraph.

A. Some people hate winter. They say it gives them colds and that they're always afraid of slipping on the ice. They even claim it makes their skin dry and red.

Other people, however, _____
_____
_____
_____

B. The newspaper printed an article about boredom. It said that many people seem to have nothing to do. They sit around complaining that life is dull. I just don't understand that. I always have more to do than I can fit in.

For example, _____
_____
_____
_____

C. There are many ways to travel, and each one has its good points and its bad points. Let's compare a few of the ways people get around.

Traveling by airplane _____
_____
_____

Traveling by car _____
_____
_____

2. On the back of this page, write a first paragraph on a subject that everyone in your class would know about, for example, recess or a popular book. Then give that paragraph to a classmate and ask him or her to write a paragraph that builds on the one you wrote.

© 1986 Monday Morning Books, Inc.

Bulletin Board

To help students recognize the importance of writing good sentences, each week select a sentence from a student's work and honor it by presenting it in large letters for everyone to read. If you include a note telling what story or paper the sentence came from, other students may wish to read that work.

ABC Sentences

GOAL:
Encouraging use of the dictionary and the thesaurus

TASK:
Write a sentence whose words come in alphabetical order. For example:

All bakers create donuts.
"A bell can ding each Friday," growled Harold.
Are both carpets dry enough?

TEACHING TIPS:
Suggest that students start with short sentences to get the feel for the activity. When they're ready to try longer sentences, use the *ABC Sentences worksheet*. Remind students that the string of words must form a real, though perhaps silly, sentence.

To make the job easier, students can use proper nouns, for example, *Harold* in the second example. They can also experiment with hyphenated words.

Be sure to keep a dictionary and a thesaurus handy.

VARIATION:
Begin anywhere in the alphabet, for example, with *g*.
Grandma Hanson, I just know, likes making nutty, orange-flavored pudding.

40

© 1986 Monday Morning Books, Inc.

ABC Sentences

Can you figure out what's unusual about the following sentence?

A bank counts dollars easily.

The words are in alphabetical order.

1. Fill in the following ABC sentences. Be sure that each one makes sense. If you like, you can use some of the words in the box:
    a, amazing, Andy's, ants, are, bragging, billowing, bunnies, calmly, can, chewed, cow, each, east, eat, everybody, friend, from, garden, Georgia, goodies, grass

A. _____ balloon _____ drifted east _____.

B. Are _____ clouds dangerous, Emma?

C. _____ big cow did _____ fresh .

D. Angry _____ could damage Esther's father's _____.

E. _____ bit constantly, disturbing _____ friend Grandma Harriet invited.

F. Apple butter _____ delight _____.

2. Complete the following ABC sentences. Each sentence should have at least three words. Make sure each ends up as a real sentence and not just a bunch of words. If you need more space, write the sentence on your own paper.

A. Ask _____.

B. Alertly, Brenda _____.

3. Make up your own ABC sentence from scratch.

© 1986 Monday Morning Books, Inc.

About-me Sentences

GOAL:
Developing categorizing skills

TASK:
Write a sentence that tells something true about yourself *and* true about every other person in the room.

> I am alive.
> My mother was born before I was born.

Now, write a sentence that tells something true about you but *not* true about anyone else in the room.

> I live at 1111 Greenwood Avenue.
> I had my appendix taken out on July 14 of last year.

TEACHING TIPS:
Model the activity before using the *About-me worksheet*. You might say, "Let me see if I can tell something about myself that is also true for everyone else in this room. Ready? *I eat food every day.* Now, put up your hand if that is true for you."

By modeling a sentence that doesn't work, you can teach the value of editing. Suppose your true-just-for-me sentence declares:

> I ate a sandwich yesterday.

If someone else did, too, you could revise your sentence, adding details that make it unique, for example,

> I ate a banana sandwich yesterday.

VARIATIONS:
1. Try the same activity but extend it to the school or, with older students, to everybody in the world.
2. Instead of autobiographical sentences, have students write biographical sentences. The task is to pick someone they know and then say something that is unique about that person.
3. You can turn the activity into a local current events project by having students tell something they did over the weekend that everyone else in the room did, or that no one else in the room did.

© 1986 Monday Morning Books, Inc.

About-me Sentences

1. Complete each sentence so that it says something true about you and true about everybody else in the room.

I eat _____.

Each morning I _____.

The day I was born _____.

I've never touched _____.

2. Complete each sentence so that it's true for you but *not* true for anybody else in the room.

I have seen _____.

In my room at home there is a _____.

Three words that I like are _____.

If I had a million dollars, I'd buy a _____

because _____.

3. Write a sentence that's true for you and true for everybody else in the room.

_____

_____

_____

4. On the back of this sheet, write a sentence that's true only for you. Draw a picture that goes with your sentence.

© 1986 Monday Morning Books, Inc.

Add-a-word Sentences

GOAL:
Learning to add details to a sentence

TASK:
Lengthen a sentence one word at a time.

    Share.
    Please share.
    Sandy, please share.
    Will Sandy please share?

TEACHING TIPS:
Demonstrate the activity on the board, inviting students to contribute words. Point out the need for adding or deleting punctuation marks as the sentence changes.

When students first try the activity themselves, have everyone start with the same word. Then compare the results.

Student 1	Student 2
Swim.	Swim.
I swim.	Swim quickly.
I can swim.	Swim quickly, Sal.
I can swim far.	Swim home quickly, Sal.
I can swim far enough.	Do swim home quickly, Sal.

Later, let students give the starter word for the class or for partners.

VARIATIONS:
1. Try building a sentence two words at a time.

    Wait.
    Please wait, Nell.
    Will you please wait, Nell.

2. Start with a long sentence and cut it word by word.

    When I'm hungry, I eat.
    When hungry, I eat.
    When hungry, eat.

3. Require that somewhere in the sequence, there must be a given kind of sentence, for example, an interrogative.

© 1986 Monday Morning Books, Inc.

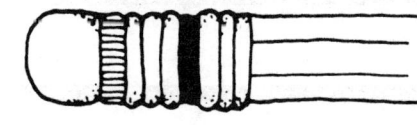

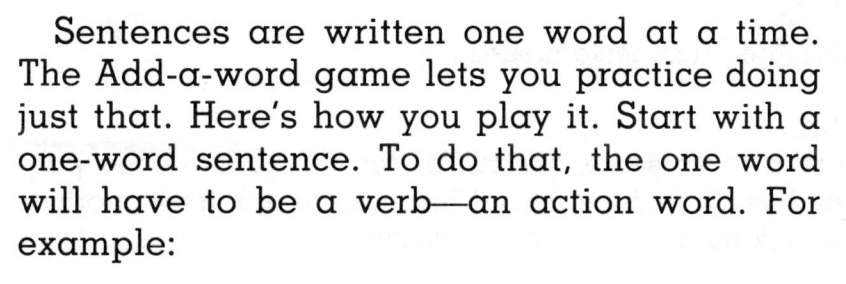

Add-a-word Game

Sentences are written one word at a time. The Add-a-word game lets you practice doing just that. Here's how you play it. Start with a one-word sentence. To do that, the one word will have to be a verb—an action word. For example:

Share.

Now, write a two-word sentence that uses *share*. For example:

Share.
Please share.

Next, try a three-word sentence.

Sandy, please share.

The idea is to see how far you can go.

Will Sandy please share?
Will Sandy please share now?
Will you, Sandy, please share now?

See if you can do it with the following word:

Run.

© 1986 Monday Morning Books, Inc.

Bumper Stickers

GOAL:
Publishing a concise message

TASK:
Write a short sentence—ten or fewer words—to be published as a bumper sticker. The sticker might give information, ask questions, or offer advice.

TEACHING TIPS:
For background, have students jot down and share bumper sticker messages they see on cars around town.

When it's time to produce bumper stickers, hand out the *How to Make a Bumper Sticker* worksheet.

Note: For professional-looking bumper stickers, show students how to letter their messages using stencils. Even better, if you have access to a computer with a banner-making program, you can use it to get impressive lettering. The stickers can then be covered with plastic wrap and attached to car bumpers with water-resistant (filament) tape of the sort used to bind parcels.

VARIATIONS:
1. Suggest that students give bumper stickers as gifts.
2. Create bumper stickers to sell as fund-raisers for school projects.
3. Produce a bulletin board of imaginary bumper stickers for the cars of movie stars and other famous people, or even for characters like Superman and the Big Bad Wolf.

© 1986 Monday Morning Books, Inc.

How to Make a Bumper Sticker

Do you have an idea that you want to share with your neighbors? One way to do it is by making a bumper sticker. Here's how.

Step 1. *Pick a subject.* Bumper stickers can be about school, pets, clubs, music, or just about anything. What will your sticker be about?

Step 2. *Write your message.* If you want people to read your sticker, use seven words or fewer. Hint: Work on scratch paper until you get just the words you want.

Step 3. *Cut a piece of cardboard about three inches high and two feet long.*

Step 4. *In pencil, print your words on the cardboard.* Make the letters at least one inch tall and half an inch wide. Use a ruler to keep the letters on a line. If you don't like the spacing, erase the letters and try again.

Step 5. *When the letters look right, darken them with crayons or felt-tipped markers.* You might even use colors.

Step 6. *Cover the bumper sticker with clear plastic wrap.* This will protect it from rain and dirt.

Step 7. *Find someone who will let you attach your bumper sticker to his or her car's bumper.*

Step 8. *Attach the sticker using plastic mailing tape.*

© 1986 Monday Morning Books, Inc.

Captions

Flydo wins the title of Best Animal Frisbee Player.

GOAL:
Sharpening observation skills

TASK:
Write a caption that helps the reader see more in a picture.

TEACHING TIPS:
Start by having students collect and read captions found in magazines and newspapers. Discuss the three jobs that a caption can do — 1) give non-visual information, such as names; 2) point out parts of the picture that the reader might overlook; and 3) explain or interpret the picture.

Have students write captions for the pictures on the *Caption Writing* worksheet.

VARIATIONS:
1. Write captions for original artwork or for pictures from family photo albums.
2. Have students write captions for illustrations included in their stories and reports.
3. Students can write captions for objects, such as coins, stamps, rocks, or toys displayed in a classroom museum. The result will be a kind of written "show and tell."
4. Have students write humorous captions that turn news photos, advertising art, and other pictures into visual jokes. Some of these jokes can also have a serious side, for example, a caption that turns a liquor ad into a parody warning about drunk driving.

© 1986 Monday Morning Books, Inc.

Captions

Captions are words that help readers understand pictures. A caption can tell about something not seen in the picture, for example, a name. It can also tell the reader what to look for.

1. Write a caption that tells something about this picture.

2. Write a caption that helps the viewer notice three or four important parts of the picture below.

_____

_____

_____

_____

3. Draw a picture on the back of this sheet. Then write a caption for the picture.

© 1986 Monday Morning Books, Inc.

49

Definitions

GOAL:
Learning to use details

TASK:
Write an original definition that explains the meaning of a word.

> A chair is a piece of furniture with a seat, a back, and four legs. It is used for sitting.

The definition must identify the category the word fits into, and then add details that explain what makes the word special:

   category: furniture

   details: seat, back, four legs, used for sitting

TEACHING TIPS:
To get across the idea that defining words is a creative activity, have students compare definitions of the same words found in different dictionaries.

The *What Is a Definition? worksheet* will help students grasp the basic elements of the format.

VARIATIONS:
1. As a current events project, have students write their own definitions for key words in news stories.
2. Have older students write simple dictionaries for younger students. These might be general interest dictionaries, or they could focus on specific topics such as food, sports, school life, or entertainment.
3. Older students can create definitions for spelling test dictations. These sentences should reveal the meaning of the given word, e.g., "The marble *column* holds up the roof."
4. Give students a nonsense word and have them write definitions for it. While the content will be made up, students should use the basic definition structure.

© 1986 Monday Morning Books, Inc.

What Is a Definition?

Just as you can write stories, you can write definitions. Every definition has two parts. The first part tells what group a word belongs to. The second part tells how the word is different from others in its group.

1. Complete the following definitions.

	group it belongs to	how it's special
A. A bird is	an animal	that flies.
B. A TV is	a machine	
C. A chair is	a piece of furniture	
D. A glove is	a piece of clothing	
E. A house is	a building	
F. An airplane is	_____	that flies through the air.
G. School is	_____	where people go to learn.
H. A spoon is	_____	for soft or liquid food.
I. A banjo is	_____	played by plucking strings.
J. Baseball is	_____	
K. A smile is	_____	

2. Pick any two words and write definitions for them.

© 1986 Monday Morning Books, Inc.

Digests

GOAL:
Practicing concise writing

TASK:
Compress a story, report, TV show, movie, or song lyric

TEACHING TIPS:
Familiarize students with digests by reading them summaries of TV shows printed in newspapers and TV magazines.

Demonstrate the activity by having the whole class co-author a digest of a familiar fairy tale such as "Goldilocks and the Three Bears." Set a target length of approximately 25 words.

Have students individually practice editing for conciseness by trying the *Word Cutting worksheet*.

VARIATIONS:
1. Have students write news briefs based on items in the daily newspaper. These digests can be posted on a bulletin board for the entire school to read.
2. Have students write digests of each day's activities for use by classmates returning from absences.
3. Have students write digests of their lessons, e.g., a digest of a chapter from the social studies or science textbook.

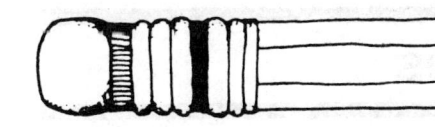

Word Cutting

Sometimes writers need to shorten what they've written.

1. Cross out one or more words from each of the following sentences, but do not change the meaning. The first one has been done for you.

A. They rode on their bicycles to school.

B. Did you open up the box?

C. We left the papers on top of the table.

D. Music was coming from out of the house.

E. Will you please warm up the soup?

F. We all looked at the picture.

G. They cleaned everything up.

2. Shorten the following sentences by replacing two or more words with one word. The first one has been done for you.

A. The robot ~~picked up~~ *lifted* the box.

B. I read a couple of books last week.

C. Everyone had gone out of the room.

D. Someone took away the glass from the shelf.

E. They got ready for the storm.

© 1986 Monday Morning Books, Inc.

Far-out Sentences

GOAL:
Learning conciseness by telling an entire story in a single sentence

TASK:
In the Paul Bunyan tradition, write a "tall tale" sentence that humorously exaggerates the truth: For example,
   My dog is so mean he's afraid of himself.
   Those basketball players are so tall, they have to get on an elevator to comb their hair.
   The fish I'm trying to catch is so big that I'm using a boa constrictor for bait instead of a worm.

TEACHING TIPS:
Familiarize students with the tall-tale brand of humor by reading folk "lies" of the sort found in books like Alvin Schwartz' two classics—*Witcracks: Jokes and Jests from American Folklore* and *Tomfoolery: Trickery and Foolery with Words.*

The *Far-out Sentences worksheet* provides some easy first-try practices with this traditional form of literary silliness.

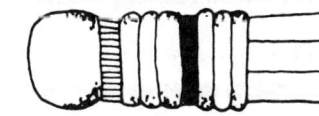

Far-out Sentences

A tall tale is a story that stretches the truth to make readers laugh. A "Far-out Sentence" works the same way.

1. Complete each of the following "tall-tale sentences." The first one has been done for you.

A. That movie was so scary _the actors ran off the screen._

B. My cat is so friendly _____

C. The band played so loudly _____

D. I was so hungry _____

E. There was so much thunder _____

F. Those basketball players are so tall _____

G. My clothes got so dirty _____

H. That painting looked so real _____

I. Yesterday was so hot _____

2. Write a few of your own tall-tale sentences on the back of this paper.

Mottoes and Slogans

GOAL:
Distinguishing between sentences and sentence fragments

TASK:
Write and display mottoes and slogans. A motto is a word, phrase, or sentence that expresses an idea for a person or group to follow. A slogan is a motto used to promote a product or company.

TEACHING TIPS:
Have students use the *Slogan Collecting worksheet* to familiarize themselves with the various forms of mottoes and slogans. That is, they will collect declarative mottoes, imperative mottoes, and so on.

Later, have students create classroom mottoes that illustrate each category:
    Complete sentence mottoes
        Declarative: Learning is our game.
        Imperative: Put your thinking cap on.
        Interrogative: Who's ready to learn?
        Exclamatory: We will succeed!

    Fragment mottoes
        Learning together
        No quitting, only trying

VARIATIONS:
1. Create mottoes for each subject area. Display the results on a bulletin board or on banners.
2. Hold a contest to create a motto for the school.
3. Create a motto for the home-school newsletter.
4. Create a motto for the PTA.
5. If there's no school system-wide motto, create one and try to get it accepted by the school board.
6. Offer a slogan-making service to local businesses.

Slogan Collecting

A slogan is a word, a phrase, or a sentence used to sell a product.

Collect at least one of each kind of slogan. You can look for slogans in newspaper and magazine ads, and in TV commercials. Tell where you found each example.

Declarative sentence slogan

Imperative sentence slogan

Interrogative sentence slogan

Exclamatory sentence slogan

Sentence fragment slogan

My Words Only Game

GOAL:
Developing word awareness

TASK:
Write a five-word sentence (the number is arbitrary) using words that no one else in the class will use. For example, if you think someone else will use *and* or *the*, then don't use these words.

TEACHING TIPS:
Invite students to flip through dictionaries while working on their sentences. But caution them to make complete sentences. Fragments such as the following don't count:
   Kangaroos, caroling quietly, haphazardly, ridiculously.
But here's one that would be allowed:
   Rockets thunder boldly skyward.

VARIATION:
As an extra challenge, require that all the words start with the same sound. For example:
   Mixed-up marooned Martians mumbled madly.

Numbered Stories and Essays

GOAL:
Learning to avoid run-on sentences

TASK:
Write a story, essay, report, or other assignment in a specified number of sentences. Here, for example, is a "Three Sentence Letter to the Editor":

> To the editor:
>
> I agree completely with last Saturday's editorial that called for a ban on thunderstorms. When I hear the booming sounds of a storm, I get dizzy. All I have to add is that we should also ban floods, earthquakes, and tornadoes.
> Sincerely,
> A.H.L.

Giving an assignment with a fixed number of sentences helps students recognize and overcome the run-on sentence problem.

TEACHING TIPS:
Demonstrate the activity on the board. Show students how to alter the number of sentences in a text by combining or by splitting sentences.

As a practice, give students a ready-made text—perhaps an article from the newspaper or a passage from a novel—which is to be rewritten in a certain number of sentences.

VARIATIONS:
1. Have students write works that consist of a set number of *paragraphs*.
2. Have students write ABC stories or essays. These are works that consist of 26 sentences. The first sentence starts with an *A* word, the second with a *B* word, and so on through the alphabet. The ABC restriction tends to evoke writing with wonderfully varied sentence structure.

© 1986 Monday Morning Books, Inc.

Part-of-speech Poems

GOAL:
Working with the parts of speech in a meaningful context

TASK:
Write a non-rhyming poem using an arbitrarily chosen parts-of-speech pattern. For example:

_____ _____ _____
adjective   noun

_____ _____ _____
adjective   adjective   adjective

_____
verb

_____ .
adverb

A wolf
Gray, cold, quiet,
Eats
Alone.

TEACHING TIPS:
Before trying this activity, make sure students understand the parts of speech.

Introduce this activity with the *Parts of Speech Poetry worksheet*. Note that it invites students to invent their own patterns which can be shared with classmates.

Challenge advanced students with more detailed requirements, for example, labeling a blank "prepositional phrase."

VARIATIONS:
1. Post a collection of parts-of-speech poems on a bulletin board with the pattern they're based on. Invite passers-by to add their work.
2. Use the same task to help students invent unusual titles for their writing, e.g., a story title that uses this pattern:

_____ . _____ . _____
verb   verb   verb

© 1986 Monday Morning Books, Inc.

Pass-it-on Sentences

GOAL:
Learning to focus on each word in a sentence

TASK:
Collaborate on the writing of a well-made sentence.
   Student 1 writes:
      Many
and passes the paper to student 2.
   Student 2 adds the next word:
      Many wild
   Student 3 continues the process:
      Many wild but

And so it goes. To keep the sentence from becoming infinitely long, require that the sentence end by the 15th word or by any other arbitrarily chosen point.

TEACHING TIPS:
Introduce the game by playing it aloud for a few times. Then, have students try it on paper, each one starting a sentence and then passing it on.

VARIATIONS:
1. Instead of having participants add a single word, you might have them each add two or three words.
2. For more pizzazz, involve other classes by sending a sentence-in-progress from room to room throughout the school.
3. Use the same technique to have students create entire stories, poems, or articles. The first student writes a single sentence, then passes the paper to another student who adds the second sentence.

© 1986 Monday Morning Books, Inc.

Single Sentence Picture Books

GOAL:
Learning to highlight every sentence in a story

TASK:
Create a children's picture book that features one sentence per page.

TEACHING TIPS:
To prepare students for writing their books, read aloud a few picture books that have only a small amount of text per page. Point out that while many picture books use more than one sentence on a page, this project calls for a single sentence.

As an easy first project, have students write the text for the eight-page story illustrated on the *You Write the Words worksheets*.

A slightly more difficult second effort might be to illustrate and retell familiar fairy tales.

When the books are done, encourage students to share them with younger children in your school, or have the school librarian catalog them for inclusion in the library.

VARIATION:
Have students write one-paragraph-on-a-page picture books.

You Write the Words

Write a sentence for each picture of the story on this page.

1	2
3	4

© 1986 Monday Morning Books, Inc.

63

You Write the Words

Write a sentence for each picture of the story on this page.

64 © 1986 Monday Morning Books, Inc.